ERRATIC
FACTS

ERRATIC FACTS

POEMS

KAY RYAN

GROVE PRESS • NEW YORK

Published simultaneously in Canada
Printed in the United States of America

FIRST EDITION

ISBN 978-0-8021-2405-0
eISBN 978-0-8021-9085-7

Grove Press
an imprint of Grove Atlantic
154 West 14th Street
New York, NY 10011

groveatlantic.com

15 16 17 18   10 9 8 7 6 5 4 3 2 1

Singular thanks to the
John D. and Catherine T. MacArthur Foundation
for their support during the writing of most of this book.

for Carol anyhow

erratic: (n) *Geol.* A boulder or the like carried by glacial ice and deposited some distance from its place of origin

Contents

ERRATIC
FACTS

New Rooms

The mind must
set itself up
wherever it goes
and it would be
most convenient
to impose its
old rooms—just
tack them up
like an interior
tent. Oh but
the new holes
aren't where
the windows
went.

On the Nature of Understanding

Say you hoped to
tame something
wild and stayed
calm and inched up
day by day. Or even
not tame it but
meet it half way.
Things went along.
You made progress,
understanding
it would be a
lengthy process,
sensing changes
in your hair and
nails. So it's
strange when it
attacks: you thought
you had a deal.

Why Explain the Precise by Way of the Less Precise?

—Timothy Eastman, *Physics and Whitehead: Process, Quantum and Experience*

It doesn't seem
right to think
blunt blows
could do a thing
like that but
we do know
arrowheads
are knapped
with rocks so
maybe it is
possible that
some kind of edge
could result from
generalized
impacts or large
blasts, a mind
grow somehow
more exact.

Ship in a Bottle

It seems
impossible—
not just a
ship in a
bottle but
wind and sea.
The ship starts
to struggle—an
emergency of the
too realized we
realize. We can
get it out but
not without
spilling its world.
A hammer tap
and they're free.
Which death
will it be,
little sailors?

MONK STYLE

In practice, it took 45 minutes to get his stride.
It was hard for Monk to play Monk.

—NPR

It may be that
Monk is always
playing Monk but
down the hall.

There are
long corridors
as in a school.

Monk must
approach himself,
join himself
at the bench
and sit awhile.

Then slip his
hands into his
hands Monk
style.

DRY THINGS

The water level
comes up when
you throw in
stones, bricks,
anything that
sinks. It's a
miracle when
that works,
don't you think?
Dry things
letting us
drink?

ERASURE

We just don't
know what
erases what
or much about
the deep nature
of erasure. But
these places with
rubbery crumbs
are exciting us
currently; this
whole area
may have been
a defactory.

AN INSTRUMENT WITH KEYS

As though memory
were not a history
but an instrument
with keys on which
no *C* would stay played
without rehitting *C*.

As though memory
were a large orchestra
without a repertoire
till it began.

Whereupon
it remembered
all of Chopin.

BRIEF REAL THINGS

He did not live in conventional order
from day to day, but grew strong
or weak like the wind.
      —David Thompson, *Wild Excursions:*
            The Life and Fiction of Lawrence Sterne

Creatures whose
habits match nothing
we understand
are untrackable by our
most implacable
trackers of air
sea and land.
As though conjured
by conditions;
as though constellations
fretted something
to existence; as though
larger arrangements—and
the trackers regret this—
produced brief real things
in real places.

HOMAGE TO JOSEPH BRODSKY

One need not smoke
to inhale. The air
in bars holds its
load of tars in
stale suspension.
Also jails. Jails
are a prison for
the person who
abhors smoke.
But happily
gorgeous thought
also hangs around
like that: you can
walk through a mist
of Brodsky and contact-
exist.

Double Floor

*. . . one sometimes does have a sense that
there is a double floor someplace . . .*
—W. G. Sebald

The dual-pupiled
frog eye can
scan for food
and trouble
above and below
the water at once.

This, like
many forms of
doubleness,
serves local
purposes

(lulling us
to the essential
focal baffling
inherent in
experience:

how the splits
keep happening).

Fizz

It may be
all there is
but we don't
understand
it: the fizz
of conversion.
Or we hope
it obtains
only in objects
or persons
not us. Or
precious to
us. A remote
effervescence
we can't like
up close. How
it works at
a surface as
though it were
false, sizzling
inside a face
until it comes
loose.

BREATHER

Maybe there
will be a
place inside
the current a
corner where
you can
recover a
rock pocket
that slowed
the water
if you were a
fish instead
of a person
with your
gills so wide
they can
see through
your head.

ALL YOUR HORSES

Say when rain
cannot make
you more wet
or a certain
thought can't
deepen and yet
you think it again:
you have lost
count. A larger
amount is
no longer a
larger amount.
There has been
a collapse; perhaps
in the night.
Like a rupture
in water (which
can't rupture
of course). All
your horses
broken out with
all your horses.

ALL YOU DID

There doesn't seem
to be a crack. A
higher pin cannot
be set. Nor can
you go back. You
hadn't even known
the face was vertical.
All you did was
walk into a room.
The tipping up
from flat was
gradual, you
must assume.

Putting Things in Proportion

The tree must be
bigger than
the house, the
doors of which
must fix upon
a width proportionate
to people. Objects
in the rooms
must coexist.
A kettle can't
be bigger than
a table. Interiors
must fit inside
in general. With
spaces left besides.
Swift justice to
rogue sizes, is what
we say—we have to
say. No one can
get along the
other way.

PLAYACTING

Something inside says
there will be a curtain,
maybe or maybe not
some bowing, probably
no roses, but certainly
a chance to unverse
or dehearse, after all
these acts. For some
fraction of the self
has always held out, the
evidence compounding
in a bank becoming
grander and more
marble: even our
most wholehearted
acts are partial.
Therefore this small
change, unspendable,
of a different metal,
accruing in a strange
account. What could it
be for but passage out?

NIGHTINGALE FLOOR

An ingenious floor, clamped and nailed in place:
walking on it caused friction between the nails
and their clamps, emitting the giveaway sounds.
There was no way to move silently on it and it had
been the shoguns' warning against spies and assassins.
        —Marshall Browne, *Rendezvous at Kamakura Inn*

Pressure anywhere
betrays betrayal: a
thousand birds awaken
from their sleep as nails.
Not patience nor
persuasion nor
dark of night
nor black costume
nor other steps taken
go an inch toward
getting past that floor
and at the shogun
who lives within his rooms
as upon an island
in the middle of a
polished wooden sea
so tuned to treachery
that sometimes
just the heat of sunlight
is misread as feet.

TOKEN LOSS

To the dragon
any loss is
total. His rest
is disrupted
if a single
jewel encrusted
goblet has
been stolen.
The circle
of himself
in the nest
of his gold
has been
broken. No
loss is token.

SALVATION

Like hope, it springs
eternal, existing in
discrete but spherical
units: a mist of total
but encapsulated
salvational events.
However if any
of these bubbles
bang against each other
no walls collapse
or double to a larger chamber,
unlike the halls of soap.

FOOL'S ERRANDS

A thing
cannot be
delivered
enough times:
this is the
rule of dogs
for whom there
are no fool's
errands. To
loop out and
come back is
good all alone.
It's gravy to
carry a ball
or a bone.

THE PAW OF A CAT

The first trickle
of water down
a dry ditch stretches
like the paw
of a cat, slightly
tucked at the front,
unambitious
about auguring
wet. It may sink
later but it hasn't
yet.

VENICE

There is a category
of person eased
by constraint, soothed
when things cease.
It is the assault
of abundance
from which they seek
release. The gorgeous
intensities of Venice
would work best
for these people
at a distance:
sitting, for example,
in a departing
train car, feeling the
menace settle.

TREADING WATER

When water
is so hard to
tread, it seems
purposely hurtful
that this is
so often said
dismissively.
With so much
paper spread
over the water's
surface, it's
incredible trouble
to paddle even
a small doglike
vertical paddle
in a circle.

FATAL FLAW

The fatal flaw
works through
the body like
a needle, just
a stitch now
and then, again
and again missing
the heart. Most
people never bend
in the fatal way
at the fatal instant,
although they
harbor a needle
they shouldn't,
or, conversely,
some critical little
lifesaving sliver
is absent.

Splitting Ice

Like standing
on splitting ice
one foot on one
one on the
other piece.
Distressed like
the family of man
at the divorce
of the plates:
some cast into
a suddenly new
world as though
having sinned;
those kept behind
trapped and
bereft. But in
a *person*, one
foot will lift
and the split
resolve. So
why do the
self-saved
feel half left?

CRISS CROSSES

(*Chiasmus*)

Even how
the crow
walks is
criss crosses
as though
each step
checked the
last. No one
knows why
he advances
as well as he
does or
could expect
that laughable
croak to work
in so many
circumstances.

LITTLE DOTS

*What else does the infinite consist of other than
the incalculability of little dots?*

—Robert Walser

The things we know
cannot be applied.
Dots, say. With dots
inside.

Walls of shelves of
jars of dots equal
one dot.

So no one is poor
nor are they lost
if they roll on the
floor.

Dragon's Teeth

Let the poet's voice lose all its measure and joints,
its character will not be changed by this; even the
fragments will be beautiful.

—Montaigne

A small wallet
of dragon's teeth
is so potent that
one wonders why
forces are raised
any other way.
The sower has a
crop of soldiers
in under a day.
Nonetheless
interest in
packets of these
pointed seeds stays
unaccountably low
across the
many fields
where they
would grow.

SHOOT THE MOON

To do it at all
we must do it
too soon: shoot
before the moon
to shoot the moon,
we learn, having
shot it dead,
bagged now and
heavy as a head.

A Kind of Life

Coins cast
from coins
in a line
going back
to the time

when the
likeness
was struck
from life:

a kind of
life itself,
it could be
argued.

The continued
evolution of
a face

becoming cruder
and more
blurred.

Bunched Cloths

Artists have
found them
endlessly beautiful:
the casually cast
or bunched cloths
after the morning
meal or lunch, how
shadows dent and dimple
the soft collapsing
tents, the human
moment past. How
linen bends in
accidental sympathy
with time perhaps
(those mirrored C's
Claesz saw and then
Cezanne again,
like laugh lines
at the corners of
time's mouth). Here
in the after time,
the empty house.

THE MAIN DIFFICULTY
OF WATER WHEELS

. . . was their inseparability from water.
—Wikipedia

There are machines of
great generative power
that can only work locally
for one reason or another.
The great fixed wheels
moved by water
cannot be moved
from water. It hurts
to think of anything
wrenched out of where
it works. But not
just for the work.
Those buckets
drenching the river,
all the ornaments
of torque.

WHY IT IS HARD TO START

A crust of jacks-
shaped interlocking
particles settles on
everything stopped.
More metallic and
angled than snow
or dust but something
like those in how
it packs. But also
like tumbleweeds,
the way they tangle
against a gate, how
you must crash
your way through,
breaking a million
little wrists. A resistance
like rip rap, too, that
thwarts tides. But small
of course, to work
inside hearts. That
pause before the next
beat starts, then that
sizzly sound? The
endless work of
overcoming; the
jacks going down.

MUSICAL CHAIRS

Only the one is
musical, actually.
The others are
ordinary, mostly
from the kitchen.
Not a peep of
music out of them
as they are taken
from rotation. Mum
chairs, tuneless
racks, dumbsticks,
next to the
escalating operatic
ravishments
of banishment
sung to the children
by the one chair
absent.

Sock

Imagine an
inversion as
simple as socks:
putting your hand
into the toe of
yourself and
pulling. Now
when you talk
you are relieved
to find your tongue
is inside out. And
when you say *I*
believe I may be
based on a different
carbon, people
are shocked
as they always
should have been.

MY KINGDOM
FOR A HORSE

Your kingdom
has already
grown abstract.

No one with an
actual kingdom
suggests a trade
like that.

It can, of course,
have been so
rapid that you
still don't know.

We have to hope
your voice will prove
the final property
to go:

of the ancestral timber
the last redoubt,
still ringing of
your great estates,

the lowliest page
of any one of which
would race to get
a horse to get
you out.

THINGS THAT HAVE
STAYED IN POSITION

Things that have
stayed in position
may nevertheless
have almost no
root system. You
could unstick
and slide them
like chess pieces.
Much of this
apparently tenacious
earth is fairly slick.

METAL

We know
in our bones
what travels.

We can act
with dispatch
if we have to.

We know
where the
silver's kept

and the blowtorch
and what else
is meltable.

Although it is
obnoxious to us

we can think
in ingots

and weigh
the precious
for metal.

Burning Tent

In the drawing
of a cell straining
laterally to split
there's no sense
that it hurts, but
why wouldn't it.
It must be as
hard to double
as half die. In
which event
an organism's
asked to reabsorb
a half gone black,
back out of systems
going blank. With
half its sufferance
denied, put out
the burning tent
and stay inside.

TRACERS

The mid-air ball
follows its arc
to the glove
in the left outfield
of the park.
There are rules.
Motion generates
projection. You
are not a fool
to believe it will
happen. Things
set a course and
follow it. The air
is full of places
where it works:
a girl and cat have
just assumed their
marks. Leading us
to think about
the dead and all
the shimmering
dots like tracers
hanging in the air
unclaimed. How
the dead can't finish
the simplest thing.

TRIPPED

The feet
are stopped
but the brain
continues its
forward motion.

Say you were a
train engine,
and a bridge
had just fallen:

Not yet even
the beginnings
of information
up from the back cars
hitting the ocean.

THOSE PLACES

They are not
imaginary but
accessible only
intermittently.

Seasonal, shall
we say, in the way
of the exquisite
high parts of
Yosemite

which
having visited
you cannot wish
inhabited
more easily.

A Trench like That

The question
is does
the sea go
exactly back
after a ship
passes. Is
a trench like
that an event
or not. Of the
vast upheaval
are there ever
final bumps and
dimples, a last
line of foam.
And where might
you think about
it from.

Almost

The mind likes
the squeeze
of chutes
and channels.

It will
go up the ramp
with cattle

pleased—almost
to the last
minute—to

almost have been
an ungulate.

VELVET

There are
hills you
long to
touch:

velvet to
the eyes.

So much
is soft

the wrong
size.

Dynamic Scaling

By using slow movements of large wings in a viscous medium,
they were able to mathematically analyze the fast movements
of tiny wings in air.
                                    —*New York Times* Science section

There are only a few
knobs: size and speed
are two. Just turn down
a bird to big and slow
and you can learn
a lot. Of course the
empyrean is now goo
which means airplanes
are caught. You see
jellied crafts not
plying the sky.
The people inside
are wondering why.

Memory Table

Even a pin
set on a
memory table
falls through.

A bare wood
kitchen table
with square legs
kicked yellow
and blue from
painted chairs
pushed in
for thirty years.

That's how little
a memory table
can do.

Nature Study: Spots

Like something
that might also
happen in the head,
they are strange
rings that flatten
and spread chalky
grey vaccination
spots on bays,
creating an exact
but dimensionless
perimeter against
the deep nap of
ferns and mosses
that coats the trunk.
All that dense life:
kept out as though
these patches were
moon or had been
bombed. Reminding us
again that live things
can be flat. And flat
can stop green things
like that.

MISER TIME

Miser time grows
profligate near the
end: unpinching
and unplanning,
abandoning the
whole idea of
savings. It's hard
to understand
but time apparently
expands with its
diminishing: the
door thrown wide
on sliding hills of high-
denomination bills and
nothing much to buy.

More of the Same

More of the same
has a telltale
splice or hitch
after the first-of-
the-same (which,
at the time,
didn't go by that
name). Things
are not quite
as fluid as we
wish, as though
there were
gaps in water,
bits of not-river;
and rivers were a
sequence of
patched fractures,
one discovered,
convincing by
speed alone like
life (ours now a
dropped dish).

The First of Never

Never dawns
as though
it were a day
and rises.

Our day-sense
says a day
can be out-waited.
So we wait.

That's the
only kind
of time
we've ever known:

it should be
getting late;
she should be
getting home.

ALBUM

Death has a life
of its own. See
how its album
has grown in
a year and how
the sharp blot of it
has softened
till those could
almost be shadows
behind the
cherry blossoms
in this shot.
In fact you
couldn't prove
they're not.

THE OBSOLETION OF
A LANGUAGE

We knew it
would happen,
one of the laws.
And that it
would be this
sudden: words
become a chewing
action of the jaws
and mouth, unheard
by the only other
citizen there was
on earth.

Party Ship

You are a
land I can't
stand leaving
and can't not.
My party ship
is pulling out.
We all have
hats. I try to
toot some notes
you'll understand
but this was not
our instrument
or plan.

BLAST

The holes have
almost left the
sky and the blanks
the paths—the
patches next to
natural, corroborated
by the incidental
sounds of practical
activities and crows,
themselves exhibiting
many of the earmarks
of the actual. This
must have happened
many times before,
we must suppose.
Almost a pulse
if we could speed
it up: the repeated
seeking of our several
senses toward each
other, fibers trying to
reach across the gap
as fast as possible,
following a blast.

Still Start

As if engine
parts could be
wrenched out
at random and
the car would
still start and
sound even,
hearts can go
with chambers
broken open.

Eggs

We turn out
as tippy as
eggs. Legs
are an illusion.
We are held
as in a carton
if someone
loves us.
It's a pity
only loss
proves this.

Pinhole

We say
pinhole.
A pin hole
of light. We
can't imagine
how bright
more of it
could be,
the way
this much
defeats night.
It almost
isn't fair,
whoever
poked this,
with such
a small act
to vanquish
blackness.

In Case of
Complete Reversal

Born into each seed
could be a small
anti-seed useful
in case of some
complete reversal:
a tiny but powerful
kit for adapting it
to the unimaginable.
If we could crack
the fineness of the shell
maybe we'd see
the bundled minuses
stacked as in a safe
and marked in ways
that, after the crash,
would spell: big bills.

STRUCK TREE

You could start
to think a struck
tree's new leaves
from up in the
good part would
turn out halves,
but you have to
laugh at yourself:
loss doesn't get
into the subsets
of absolutely
everything.

Erratic Facts

[It] was a very bizarre, erratic fact.
—W. G. Sebald

Like rocks
that just stop,
melted out
of glaciers.
Often rounded
off—egglike
sometimes
from erasure.
As though
eggs could
really be
made backwards,
smoothed from
something
stranded
and angular.
And let's think
it's still early
in the work,
and later
the eggs
will quicken
to the center.

Grateful acknowledgment is made to the following publications in which many of these poems first appeared: *Agenda* (UK); *The Believer*, *Cordite* (Australia); *Dark Horse* (UK); *Granta*, *The New Yorker*; *The North* (UK); *Parnassus*; *Poetry*; *Poetry London* (UK); Poets.org; *The Smithsonian*, *Threepenny Review*, *Virginia Quarterly Review*, *Yale Review*.